A Separated Love

Life with an Incarcerated Loved

One

Leah Rogers

Containing contributions by

Sarah Walker

J-Nae Knisley

Daisy Martinez

Nicole Muddiman

Tammie McDermott

Elizabeth Carnes

Jerri Crawford

Cover by Alex Garzes

Table of Contents

Dedication and Special Thanks

This book is dedicated to Gannie, the only mother I ever had, who loved me beyond measure and taught me that I could do anything I truly put my mind to.

To my children: Adin, Rebekah, Bailea, Azlea, and Everlie, you guys have been the loves of my life. Blue, thank you for the good times that we have shared over the years. ILY, husband.

Thank you to the ladies that submitted their stories to share, the people that completed surveys to help me, and TVR for allowing me to help support other women through their journeys.

Thank you, Sarah, and all of the ladies of the Visiting Room.

One last thank you goes to Alex for his beautiful depiction of my concept. You took my basic idea and made it more than I ever imagined. Amazing work!

Prologue

I am in a relationship. My husband being in prison doesn't make it any less of a marriage than other "normal" marriages. — Anonymous

As she peeked through her eyelids, she could see a sliver of dawn's light coming through the dark blue shimmering curtains that separated her world from the outside. She heard a familiar buzzing in her ear coming from her phone. Beep, Beep, Beep, Beep. As she picked up her cell phone, she cautiously flipped it over and saw "ALARM 5:45" flashing on the screen.

As had become typical, she didn't get much sleep the night before, but she knew that it was time for her day to begin. There were two kids to get off to school, breakfast to cook, a dog to feed, the kitchen to clean, and a couple of bills to pay before she went to work in a couple of hours. There was so much to do, and only one person to make sure it was done.

The children were sometimes difficult to get up in the morning. Her son, Adam, was 13. At 13, he took on some responsibility. Adam fed the dog most mornings. He picked out his own clothes and got himself dressed on time. He made sure his homework was done and cleaned some around the house, but he still depended on his mother to wake him for school. Waking up a 13-year-old boy is never an easy task.

The girl had long tassels of golden hair that came down to the middle of her back and loved all things My Little Pony, but she still relied on her mom for most things. At just 7, Janie enjoyed being at school but dreaded waking up most mornings. Her mom always tried to give her a little extra time to shake the sleepy dust off of her before she had to begin her day.

Monday through Friday was always so hectic, but Saturday-Saturday was their special day. On Saturdays, the mom and her children got up earlier than every other day. They put on some of their best clothes. All three of them gathered in a car to leave just after dawn. They usually stopped for a snack just before getting on the freeway. They were gearing up for a four-hour drive. First, they took the freeway, and then they drove through a few rural towns. They knew that they needed to get there early.

While other families were spending Saturdays sleeping nestled in their beds, the Miller family- Sarah, Adam, and little Janie- always spent the day with the most important man in their lives. They always went to visit Jeremy, their husband and father. Because processing took so long, the last 3 years had taught them that the earlier they got there, the better things would be.

First, they waited in the processing line with the other women, children, mothers, fathers, and others. They would empty their pockets, have their finger tips and hands swabbed, take off their shoes, and walk through a metal detector. Then they would have their ID's checked and have their pictures used to verify their ID's.

They were then led down a long hallway and through several gates with some of the other people. While the loud buzzers and the heavy gates slamming behind them were always hard on them mentally and emotionally, they accepted it as a part of the process. They would eventually make their way to the gym and pick a table. The Millers had a table that they normally sat at. They liked it because of its proximity to the vending machines and concession. As Janie and Adam would sit down at their table, Sarah would get their refreshments. She knew what everyone liked. She sat everything down on the table when she was done. Then she would start to look, listen, and wait for Jeremy to come out. That's when the clock would start. They would soak up every little moment of the next four hours: the sound of his voice, the smell of him, and the looks that he gave. They took in everything because they cherished this time. Everyone that was visiting their loved ones cherished that time. That's the way visitation was at the state prison.

-Sarah's story is one that many women across the globe can connect with.-

Introduction

This book contains the stories of eight different women from different areas of the US and Europe. As different as their lives have been, they have one thing in common: they each have a loved one that is currently or has recently served time in prison. These are their stories of difficult circumstances, love, strength, and hope.

Stop asking "How do you do it? " Just because I CHOOSE to be with a man that's incarcerated doesn't give you the right to say he's a bad man. — Stacey

Nicole

It's not easy, but I'm where I need to be. - Jen

Our story began almost two years ago with a joke email that was sent initially in search of a friend. I know that some people will be thinking "yeah, she's 'that' girl. She's one of those so desperate for male attention that she goes looking for it on the other side of the world, and in someone behind bars no less." Well, I'm not "that" girl. I'm Nicole, girlfriend to one of the most amazing men I have ever met. The first time I read his words in that first email I knew he was going to change my life. I just didn't know how yet.

I should tell you when we first started corresponding, I was married and living with my husband at the time. I had fallen out of love with him a long time ago and never really had the courage to leave. The emails flew back and forth between us, and I found myself laughing, smiling and happy for the first time in years. I also felt scared. I knew I was falling for this man, and I didn't know what to do.

I reached out to a Prison Wives forum for advice. I got some interesting responses. It was at this point that I learned not all prison wives are supportive. I had some really negative comments thrown my way. I also had a few ladies message me who I have become really good friends with, and they are the ones who help me through. They had been in this situation before and knew exactly what to say to help me through all the emotions I was feeling.

When he first told me he loved me, I cried. I had been waiting to hear it for so long. In reality, it had only been a few weeks. I fell for him hard and so quickly. He made sure to say it in a way where I actually had to ask him if that's what he meant! That's when we became a couple- 23rd November 2015. I have never been as happy as I am now in my entire life. I left my husband the same day I told Paul I loved him.

I know that people think I'm crazy, and I also know that people think I'm being used. They couldn't be more wrong. To begin with, I send him no money at all. He won't let me. All I pay for is an $8 a month fee to have an American phone number diverted to my cell phone. I forgot to mention that I live in the UK. Yeah, that's right. I'm a Brit dating an American inmate.

You are probably wondering what my family thinks. My mum has been amazing. She is so happy for me and really likes Paul. My brother and sister in law have been so supportive and also love him. My dad is skeptical. He doesn't understand how I can be in love with a man I have never met. I have tried to tell him but he's old school. He is supportive in the sense that if I'm happy then so is he. He also said to me that he hasn't seen me this happy for years. That's about as much of an approval as I'm likely to get out of him!

I will tell you, this life isn't easy. I don't get to visit. I have been rejected twice. I keep trying but they can't do a background check on me because I'm not an American citizen. I can't call him when I'm upset about something or just because I need to hear his voice. We rely on emails, letters, and two phone calls a week. On special occasions, we talk more but that's it.

It can be lonely sometimes. I have days where I just cry because I want to see him so much. Not knowing from one day to the next whether he will be on lockdown is hard. I know that if I haven't gotten any emails through by a certain time, something has happened. I hate that his attorney has approached the prosecution twice about an early release, and he has been turned down both times because they still think he is "a piece of shit". I hate that sometimes the phones are down but they still take his money and minutes even if we can't hear each other. I hate that I sometimes spend hours, even days making him something special for his birthday for them to send it back to me for no reason other than they can't be bothered to "inspect" it.

But, do you know what? None of that matters. I have this man who I love so much. He is my best friend, partner, my other half, and soul mate. He makes my life better in so many ways. He picks me up when I feel down, comforts me with words that mean so much when I feel like the world is ending, and makes me laugh so much that my face aches.

This is the man that I love: the man that will go without commissary just so he can send me extra emails and that spent a small fortune to send me a stuffed pug toy for Valentine's Day. He's a man that sent me a necklace with matching earrings because they had pink gems in them that reminded him of how beautiful I look wearing pink eye shadow. This is a man that has never failed to send me a "date" via email every Saturday.

All these hardships we face with an incarcerated loved one are overshadowed by the wonderful men we have by our sides because they ARE with us always. They are in our hearts. They will one day be by our sides. That wait is worth it. I have 3 years left to wait for my man and every single minute of it will be so worth it.

It's hard because you want to start your life NOW, but at the same time it's easy because you just KNOW that he is worth the wait. - Rhonda

Tammie

It's so hard with my kid being in jail. I raised a person, and then I lost them

to the system. - Anonymous

Overall it has been very difficult having a son in prison. It's affected my life in every aspect. Everyday living is different than it was before my son was locked up. Having a son in prison also takes a toll on your personal relationship with your spouse and is hard on me financially.

It hasn't just affected me financially. It has also exhausted me emotionally. His first time in prison, I almost had a nervous breakdown. He is currently on his fourth incarceration.

Our relationship has changed since he first went to prison. Despite the difficulty and stress of it all, we are much closer now than before. As his mother, I am his biggest supporter. I support him in every way I can.

He needs a lot of emotional support to keep his head up. Through his time in prison, he has missed the birth of both of his babies. That alone has been incredibly difficult.

I visit him as often as I can. He is permitted to have visitation every fourteen days for two hours. That time is spent talking to him about the things that he needs to talk about in person. I also talk to him every day on the phone at least once a day. He needs to be able to call so that I can just tell him that I love him.

It's taken some time, but he has finally accepted that he is the one that couldn't follow probation's rule, and now he has to accept the consequences. At first, he blamed everyone else for his being in there so I have helped him deal with that.

I also support him financially so that he can have more to eat in addition to what the DOC serves because he stands 6'10" and weighs 230 lb. The calories that they give them are not enough to fill him up. I take this burden on every month so he has enough to eat.

If he goes without me telling him I love him every night, he starts to get down on himself. When that happens, it's me and my husband who have to work to bring him back up. I also put money on the phone so he can call me every night. It also helps me emotionally.

Elizabeth

It truly makes me a strong woman. - Lona

The universe works in strange and mysterious ways. We think with our brain, but we live by our heart. The heart wants what the heart wants, and when you find "The One" nothing matters; not time, distance or separation. Everyone has their own opinions on the matter. There's a lot of judgment and doubt. None of that matters. What matters is that you love him and he loves you. It's that plain and simple. So let's begin with a little back story of my personal situation.

When I first moved to Texas in 2010, I met Russell. He was with another woman at the time that he ended up marrying. I was instantly attracted to him. What can I say? I'm a sucker for a bad boy with tattoos. He had a girl though and she and I were friends so I let it be. He ended up going to prison for 2 years in 2011. While in prison, his wife at the time cheated on him quite publicly.

When he was released in 2013, our paths crossed again. This time he was single and so was I. However he was scared to get into any sort of committed relationship, so he wanted us just to be "friends with benefits", so that's what we did. It worked for a while. No strings attached. We weren't supposed to catch "feelers" as he referred to them.

Well, he did well at staying out of trouble for a while, but then he got locked up in the county jail. Prior to this, he and I had kind of stopped talking because he was getting into trouble that I wanted no part of. One day I decided to write him a letter while he was in jail just checking up on him, and on July 31, 2014, he wrote me a letter that changed the rest of my life. He apologized for all his wrong doings and told me he should have been with me from the start. I was the girl he wanted and needed. He said he wouldn't ask me to be his girl from behind those bars, but asked if I would give him a chance when he got out. I had waited long enough and did not care if he was locked up. He wanted me, and I wanted him. We were then officially a couple.

He spent about 3 more months in there until I bonded him out, and the night he was released I moved in with him. Our life has been a crazy roller coaster ever since. I was told by others that he was no good for me, a bad influence, and this may have been true, but I was not leaving this man for anything.

He went through another lock up in county jail for 6 months, and I held him down the whole time. I wrote letters, sent pictures, went to visit every weekend. I paid for phone calls and put money on his books. I was heartbroken that he was gone. My world was shattered, but we survived.

When he came home our relationship was better than ever. In February 2016, we had a relapse. He was booked on his third felony drug charge. While out on bond 2 weeks later, he caught his

4th DWI but was taken to the hospital and never went to jail. He was released to the house. We were sure a warrant would be put out within the week. Time went by, and it wasn't until July that a warrant finally popped up for him. He turned himself in on July 14, 2016. He signed on 5 years of TDC time.

My world fell apart. I was left with rent and other bills to pay and my main provider was gone. There is no handbook on how to be a prison wife. You have to figure it out as you go. He was transferred so far away that visiting has been almost impossible for me. I had to get a landline so he could call. I learned about things like Eccom packs and J-pay. I wait for the mail to come every day. I've made parole packets and written support letters. It's all part of the package.

I got questioned by many people. They would ask, "Are you going to stay with him?" or "How can you wait that long for him?" Five years with no sex is not for the weak. I waited 24 years of life to find my soul mate, so even if he had to do 50 years, I'd wait for him.

What are five years compared to the rest of our lives? We want to have babies and grow old together. He was God's gift to me, and when God gives you a gift you do not return it.

We don't fight with each other. We support each other and praise each other for the accomplishments we continue to make. I encourage him to stay strong and not let that place turn him into a bad person. I cherish the small things like handmade cards and prayers he writes for me.

We don't sugar coat anything and I do not keep him in the dark on anything going on in the free world. I beg him to behave so he has a better shot of coming home sooner. We are living in two different worlds, and I have no idea what it's like for him in there. Since I don't know what it's like, I try not to get angry when he gets into fights or get write ups and his privileges taken away.

Days without him are hard. The nights are harder, but with each day that passes without him, that means its one day closer to him coming home. The little things are what matter. I write him every day just so he feels like he was there that day. I include the details of what happened and send him lots of pictures so he can relive the memories we share.

Love, honesty, loyalty, and respect are the keys to surviving a prison sentence. While he's in there doing his time, I'm out here doing mine. If your relationship can survive a prison sentence, it can survive ANYTHING. It's scary, heartbreaking, and stressful, but the day he walks out those doors and is a free man, it will all be worth the wait, and we can finish our happily ever after.

It's very hard. Making the choice to stand by them is not one that should be taken lightly. You both have to work extra hard to make it work. - Teresa

Jerri

For those that think "you do the crime, you do the time"; realize that when you put a father or son behind bars, the people that are hurt the most are the wife and children and parents. We committed no crime, and no one ever mentions their concern for us. - Michelle

I support my daughter by mail, phone and money. It's so surreal knowing she has to be away for 27 years. I pray I will still be here on this earth for her when she is paroled. I don't see her often as I would like as she is 12 hours away. I send cards of encouragement and she tries to ease my mind that she is ok. She's 29 and the rest of her adult life will be incarcerated. We pray and rely on faith that this too will pass.

Sarah

I didn't choose this path for us, but the situation has made us value each other

that much more. — Shannon

Like most people, I never thought I'd be a prison girlfriend. So how did I get here?

One day in 2012 I was binge watching a prison "reality" program and decided that I would reach out to inmates to become friends. It was a good deed I told myself. These are people who need friends, someone to lean on, someone who tells them their mistakes are okay and they are deserving of kindness and compassion. I thought that person to provide these things was me. The next few days were spent reviewing profiles on a prison pen pal website and I had a total of five potential pen pals selected. My selection process was simple; someone around my age, who was not in my state and who had a long sentence who didn't sound overly romantic in their profile, because I was just interested in being friends, right?

The initial letters back and forth were very mundane, much like any small talk between two strangers who are getting to know each other. After a few weeks, one pen pal asked for some money, I responded and told him no, he never wrote back. Shortly after that, another asked for some suggestive pictures, I wrote him back and told him no, he never wrote back but in turn threw my letters in the trash where another inmate found them and reached out. I looked up his case and responded to ask him to not contact me again. Now I was down to three inmates, New York, California and Texas. Over the next few months, my New York friend and I began to correspond more frequently. We wrote about gender issues, nature, science, of course, prison and the reason he was there.

I'm not sure what happened, but at one point something happened, not something exciting or big, but just something and I wanted to tell New York. That night I began to look into how to get phone calls from prison and set up a landline with my phone company. The next day or so I got a letter from him, it was a quick note in response to something I had sent via an app to see if that was faster because it was taking a week to get a letter there and a week back. His note said, "Got your card, not sure if it was faster. Maybe we can talk on the phone?" Of course, I immediately responded with my new number and then I waited. It took a week.

While I waited, the apartment upstairs from me flooded and my bedroom ceiling caved in from the weight of the water, the only phone jack was in my bedroom, so the room consisted of construction materials and a phone. On Tuesday, the phone rang. My heart jumped into my throat, I had butterflies and my hands were shaking as I answered. Our first conversation was full of giggles and small talk, much like the first few letters. The thirty minutes blew by and then it was over. He said he might try to call the next week, I said okay. He called the next night.

Those were the good days when he had a porter job and we could talk almost every day and for an hour Saturday and Sunday. He kept telling me how spoiled I was. After talking on the phone for a few weeks I knew I liked him. It came to me as I opened my refrigerator one day to get out some milk. The next time we spoke I asked him if I could come and meet him. I started planning and a few days later at work, I got a bonus that was the amount of my trip. I was starting to believe the universe was telling me something.

I spoke with my family about New York.

His name is Daniel.

When Daniel was 17, he was stealing a car. The car owner came out of his home to stop Daniel, and he shot him. Daniel was arrested and pled guilty. He received a sentence of 20 years to life. Years later, a childhood acquaintance implicated him in the death of Daniel's childhood friend who had gone missing in the mid-1990's. Daniel was found guilty and currently is working towards appealing this conviction.

Some days they were more supportive than others. In the end, my family's concern is with my happiness. I think due to the length of his sentence there are some existing concerns about long term happiness, but that is the nature of life I suppose. You never know how things will work out until it does.

Anyway, my trip was getting closer. Our phone calls had become more negotiations on how to have a relationship of this nature. We would spend an entire click (slang for a phone call) discussing how we would handle arguments and what kind of future we wanted. Then the recording would come on to let us know that it was time to end the call and he would give his customary, "Stay outta trouble and take care of yourself" and the call would end.

As I left for New York, I didn't know what would happen. We had agreed not to talk about things until we were sitting there together. I told him that I was clumsy, he said it was okay. He asked around to get information for what I could expect as far as processing goes and put me in touch with a friend's wife who I could ask questions. My cab ride to the prison the first day was nerve racking. When I got there, I walked in and announced that I was new and had no idea what I was doing. The correctional officers looked at me and helped me out. It was a Thursday, so there wasn't really a line but if there was, it didn't matter because I was the first one there.

Once I was finished in processing and was assigned my seat I waited. I nervously waited. I watched other women go to the vending machines and get all kinds of snacks. I asked myself over and over what I was doing. There was a door in the corner behind me which kept opening and some new man would walk out and go check in and go to his waiting person. I didn't even hear it when

Daniel walked in, but I heard him say my name when he walked up to our table.

That first day was like our first phone call on steroids. Here we are, both over 30 years old and still giggling every time we make eye contact. He had sent me pictures of himself obviously, but his smile in person is the most amazing smile I've ever seen. At one point, he leaned over the table and it startled me because it was so abrupt that I turned my head, then paused and kissed my cheek. I spent the next two hours trying to figure out how I could get him to try to kiss me again, because damn... I really wanted to taste that smile.

The second day was the last day for that trip. About midway through the day, we decided to have the talk, kind of. Remember the lunge? The night before I, texted the prison wife I knew and told her about it and schemed on how I could get him to try to kiss me again, because damn it I was not kissing him first. She, in turn, spoke with her husband, who told Daniel, so he knew.

The next day, I asked him, "So, that thing you did yesterday, over the table, were you trying to kiss me?" He laughed and nodded. Then I suggested he try it again. It was seriously the most awkward kiss I've ever had. We both started laughing in the middle of it and stopped. Then we tried again and everything else faded away. For a few brief moments, it was just us alone sharing this moment. Eventually, a guard came by to let us know we needed to calm down and we went back to our giggling. I asked him how he felt about me, he said: "Maybe I might love you." I said, "Oh, I might love you too." That is how we left it. I was flying out in the morning and was going to stay with some other family for a few days before I'd get home so we could talk again.

It was nearly a week before we spoke again. I caught him up on my trip with my family and what had been going on at work. We talked about how wonderful it was to see each other and discussed when I might come up again. I asked, "So.... Are you my boyfriend now or what?" He paused and responded with, "Yea. I guess so!" The thirty minutes zoomed by, when the recording came on instead of his normal spiel, he said "I love you" followed by "gosh... doesn't that just feel great? I've spent the past month or so wanting to say that before we hung up and now it's out there."

We settled into a routine. He would call every day or every other day and I would visit every three or four months the first year or so. Then he was transferred into a program he needed if we were to get married and get family visits. My good old days of being spoiled and having hours of conversation were shortened to one or two 30 minute phone calls a week. I hated it, but it was out of his hands.

We got engaged after dating for about a year. He asked me at a visit and I said yes. A few weeks after I returned, my job fired me. Daniel blamed himself. I never hid him. I never felt a reason to. People make mistakes, people make huge mistakes. I decided to use my time unemployed to go to college and work part time. As a potential wedding date drew nearer, I could hear some apprehension in his voice whenever we talked about getting married. Finally, I asked him what was going on. He felt bad about the hardships I was going through and he was worried if we got married that it could just make life harder for me. I said I didn't care, I loved him and I wanted to marry him. He said he couldn't deal with that guilt. So we did not get married.

It was a sore topic for a while between us. It still is, just to a lesser degree. By him not wanting to get married it removes the opportunity for us to get family visits, which we might not have been approved for anyway due to the nature of his convictions. Why am I still here? It is simple, he wasn't willing to risk my future on the chance that he might get laid. He knows I had things I wanted to do that it is unlikely I would be able to if we had been married. I stay because there isn't a single thing anyone can say or show me to convince me that Daniel hasn't been looking out for what he believes is in my best interest. I didn't always feel that way about it, for a while I was really bitter. Then one day, after a visit, I was waiting for a cab and I was crying and this guy who was visiting his son came up and started talking with me. I told him how mad I was about the getting married thing and he pointed out of selfless Daniel was being and how many men use getting married as a way to have someone to sleep with without thinking of the consequences for the woman involved.

That was two years ago. These days things have a new normal for us. We talk a few times a week, though I long for the good ol' days where we talked more frequently. However, since the escape at Clinton in 2015, phone calls are limited to 15 minutes and are regulated by the guards in the yard. Occasionally, we will get a full click in, but it is more common to get a quick five-minute call when there are a few spare moments to touch base and to say our I love you's. That sounds rough, but we still have it pretty good. We still have letters and get to hear each other's voice. As is the nature of life: some times are harder than others and I find comfort in unloading in my letters to him and rereading past letters.

If there is one thing I've learned it is that respect and honesty are the most important aspects of a relationship. I hear people say communication a lot, but I think without respect and honesty the communication between people in a relationship is pointless. We are grateful for the things we do have in each other and focus on those things rather than in what the other person is lacking at that specific moment. I think part of what sets us apart is that we are both a bit introverted and understand sometimes we just need time to ourselves. Daniel is always encouraging me when I am pursuing things that are for my betterment, and I do the same for him even when I don't understand them, like him and sports.

All relationships take work, like real work. You need to be on the same team, even when things suck. Sometimes things can suck for a long time for one of you, or both of you, but if you want it to work, you will try to figure it out. Daniel and I certainly don't always agree and more often we agree to disagree about something. Back when we were still in negotiations, we talked about what would make us want to break up with the other person; he said if he couldn't trust me or if we spent more time fighting than enjoying ourselves. There have been a few times when we've asked each other how we were doing as a team. What can we do differently? How can our relationship evolve and grow? Should our relationship end? I think it's important to ask these questions and to get the answers, but be ready for answers you don't like and instead of being offended when you don't like them perhaps take a second to realize the person you're in a relationship with is a human being too and who has their own things going on. In short – your partner's life, inmate or not, does not revolve around you and your happiness.

A few weeks ago, I watched some YouTube video that had wedding vows in it. I listened to the bride's vows to her husband and rolled my eyes and thought, "What a bunch of bullshit" so I took a few minutes and wrote some vows to Daniel. What pissed me off was that it seemed like a bunch of false promises like and silliness like I'm so happy you chose me and I'll never stop being the girl you fell in love with, it just seemed fake. So, being the romantic that I am I decided to write some vows for the wedding we never had. A few days later he called and I read them to him:

"Daniel, do you remember before how we met I said I might trip over my own feet? You reassured me that I would be okay, but I did trip as I stood to greet you. I tripped but I didn't fall into your arms, instead I was able to catch myself as I fell in love with you. This has been a reoccurring theme in our relationship, I get anxious and full of doubt in myself and you redirect me and help me remember how strong I am. You push me into being a better person for me. You forced me to see things in myself that I refused to see. You push me to do what makes me happy even when that means risking your own happiness. You've told me several times that all you want for me is happiness and while that's a cliché things most people say, when you say it you're being completely genuine. You've taught me what real love is. I don't have a list of promises for you, only one. I promise I will always try to be the best version of myself for you. I love you."

When I finished, there was silence for a moment and then, "Ah, babe. Thank you. I love you. I wish I could just hold you right now."

The point is that relationships mature and change. They must because the people involved in them grow. I know we want to cling onto the feelings of those phone calls from when we first met when it was all new and discovering each other, but after a time you're at a new undiscovered country that is full of unknowns. In a lot of ways, I think that we have it better than some couples who are not in this situation because we are forced to have meaningful interactions with each other as opposed to just tuning into a television show and not talking about things. Don't get me wrong, I'd love nothing more than to sit and watch some Game of Thrones with Daniel, but not at the cost of losing the dialogue we have.

Tomorrow or the next day, Daniel will call. We will get caught up on each other's news and then say I love you. It still feels good.

The struggle is real, but staying positive is the best medicine. — Jenn

Daisy

I'm not stupid or naive. I'm in love and I trust that man with me entire soul.

Don't judge unless you've walked in my shoes.

No matter how happy you are someone will always have something negative to say. I've learned how to side step those comments and "concerns" other people might have. I know it might sound a little cliché, but I truly feel like I married my best friend or at least one of them. Something about him was completely different from any man I'd ever met. What was weird is that he told me the exact same thing about me.

It began with just flirtation. He was very funny with the same demented, sarcastic sense of humor as me but only with me. With others he was very cold and quite. Before we got together, I knew of him but never talked to him. But it's very true what they say about timing being everything. It just wasn't our time yet. I have a 5 year old from my previous relationship and in that relationship I never felt like myself. I genuinely feel like the only reason I meet my daughter's dad was to create our daughter but we were never meant to be together. I was always trying to be who he wanted me to be, suppressing who I really am. And with My husband I'm truly me.

The way he knows me is amazing- from my tone of voice facial reactions and even to the point where in he gets a sick feeling in his stomach when something is wrong with me. And, he makes sure to get a hold of me to find out what's going on. I've never had a love like this.

I grew up in Pomona, California. Yes, it's a rather ghetto area. I grew up with gang members. My childhood dream was to marry someone like who I grew up with. In my eyes, those men were always the protectors. I saw myself with three or four children, a modest little home, and my protector by my side.

I finally feel like that's where I'm headed but just taking the road less traveled, and I can see why it is. No one wakes up and says "Hey I'm going to fall in love with this guy that's in prison and make my life a lot more difficult." I understood everything that came along with wanting to be with him but at the end of it all, I got him so it was worth it.

The first few days when we began talking, he asked me "So when are we getting married?" I laughed it off and thought this guy was ridiculous. I could not believe what he was asking me. I thought he was joking. The joke's on me as I sit here baring his last name now. The stigma of marrying someone in prison is kind of scary because, let's be honest, at one point or another some of us have sat back and questioned our decision. I will never lie about that, but when I did start I always had a sign.

The best sign was the day we got married, up until the day we got married my daughter had never physically been around him. All of our visits were always behind glass, although almost every time I didn't bring her, they would accidentally let him have contact visits. I love new staff when they commit human errors. She was never was able to touch him until the day that we got married. They took him out from behind the glass for the ceremony, and the moment he walked through the door, he kneeled down and opened his arms. My daughter ran to him with no hesitation. She threw herself at him, and the way they looked together was like he had been her father all along. If ever I had a doubt in my heart, that moment made it vanish. Visits, lock downs, 15 minute phone calls, letters, and pictures with horrible backgrounds are how we are currently living, but soon it will be a thing of the past. Next year my husband will be graduating with an associate's degree in Social Sciences. We have many letters of recommendation for when it's time to go see the parole board in 3 years, and we're patiently waiting for our first family visit. Yes, we will be trying for our second child, and I couldn't be happier.

This life is not for everyone and that's okay. It's a lifestyle that is not easy. —

Anonymous

J-nae

I know the real person not just the inmate. - Maria

My significant other, Mark, has been in prison since 2010. His minimum is in 2022. We were not always together, but I've been riding this out with him since the day he went in. I've known him for 11 years, and we have a complicated history, but long story short, I've always had feelings for him outside of just being friends. I found out that he had been arrested because his story was local front page news. Immediately upon reading the article, I wrote him a letter.

The longer we wrote, talked on the phone, and spent time together at visits, the more I learned about him, and the stronger my feelings got. I was in another relationship for 5 years of Mark's sentence. There were many tears and heartache during that relationship, and Mark was there for me through all of it. He was like my "dear diary" and knew every awful thing that happened. I left nothing out, and he was the only person that I trusted like that.

Toward the end of that other relationship, I was cheated on pretty blatantly, and I was devastated. Before that, Mark had never even suggested or encouraged me to leave outright. He had always said I deserved better, but this time, he straight up said I needed to reevaluate my life and get out of that situation because it was making me miserable. Though I didn't take that advice right away, I told Mark that I would. I began to prepare myself for the break-up. It took me months, and Mark was very patient. During that time, we started talking about being together officially and even talked about getting married. Eventually, when I got the courage and had officially had enough, I ended that relationship and almost immediately started a new one with Mark.

Starting a relationship with Mark just felt like coming home. It felt like it was a long time coming, and Mark had even said at one point, "we can keep doing this little dance we've been doing for almost a decade, or we can just be together and see what happens." That was a perfect description of how it went for us. Despite his incarceration and the restrictions that come with it, I know that this man is the man I'm supposed to spend my life with.

I've always known I had feelings, but I was afraid that he didn't have them in return and that he would reject me. I didn't want to lose his friendship – a friendship that I had begun to depend on over the years. Plus, I kept asking myself, "Who would choose to be with a man in prison? Would I be able to wait for him faithfully for six years and possibly more if he's not paroled on time? What if he's different when he comes home? Even worse, what if he's not different? What if he goes back?" The truth is that stuff really matters, and it's a lot to take in when thinking of getting into a situation like this, or worse, being thrown into it without warning like so many other ladies are.

I chose to tell Mark the truth about how I felt, and I chose to be with him because I have never loved or trusted someone more. No one has ever made me feel more loved and appreciated than he does. I know it probably sounds strange to someone who has never experienced it, but when you're in a situation such as this one, you have to rely on your mental and emotional connection with your significant other to make things work. Visits are only once per week – the rest of the time, the communication happens through phone calls, emails, and letters.

I am very lucky to be able to visit Mark every weekend. I drive two hours each way to do so. I get to sit beside him, hold him and be held. We hold hands and kiss and I rub his head and his back how he likes. A quirky thing that I enjoy that people don't generally understand is that I like for him to bite me – just on my upper arm or shoulder - and leave a bruise every week. By the time that bruise is healing, it's time to go back and get a new one. It is oddly comforting to me because it's like I get to take something that he gave to me and bring it home.

I put money on a vending card for the vending machines – about $25 per visit – and he can eat subs or sandwiches and junk food, drink sodas or tea and coffee. I never eat while I'm there because I feel guilty about taking food away from the inmates. I can eat good food anytime. They can only eat it during visits. My visits are more liberal than most; from what I've learned from other prison wives and I am endlessly grateful for that.

We have decided to get married while he's in there, as well. We've met some resistance from the prison, but we are waiting until next year to push the issue. The denials are related to a write-up that he got for hanging a curtain in his window – a curtain that he bought from commissary. Despite this not falling under the "reasons for denial" in the marriage policy, both the original request and the appeal were denied. His counselor is very unhelpful and unprofessional. She threatened that she would take me off of his visiting list if I were to contact her about the denial. The things that the staff at some of these facilities does are just outrageous to me. It not only hurts the inmates but the people who love them as well. If we have to get through this sentence to live the life that we want, then so be it, because there's no one else in the world that could take his place.

We write so many letters and send so many emails. I am starting my 5th binder full of mail from him. We've gotten creative with letters. He started writing a story over a year ago for me to continue writing, and the story is still going strong. We're the main characters, of course! We've spilled so many secrets about ourselves in those letters and literally put our hearts on the pages. It is reminiscent of old-school love stories, and I enjoy that very much.

I've always liked to write, so I think Mark got lucky with me there. He has also opened himself up in ways that he never has with anyone before me, and I feel lucky to know the man that he is and everything that he's always bottled up. I think that, without letters, neither of us could have been so open with each other in the beginning. That openness has now carried over into all other forms of communication, and our relationship is thriving because of it.

As for emails, they are limited to 2,000 characters each. They don't always go through quickly – especially on weekends. Sometimes emails that are sent on Friday nights aren't received until Monday morning or early afternoon due to security reviews at the prison. We have just begun using song titles and artists for the subjects since we were running out of original ideas. The rule is, we can't use the same song twice. It should get interesting, being that we exchange about six emails per day and he has 1,710 days left until his minimum parole date as I write this. That's a lot of music!

Phone calls are inconsistent. There was a time that Mark could and would call me between six and eight times per day. Phone calls for us are 99 cents for 15 minutes. There was also a time that Mark had to sign up for a time slot on the phones every day, and during that time we rarely talked on the phone at all.

Right now, he can pretty consistently call twice a day – after his lunch before they lock in for afternoon count, and then after he gets off of work before they lock in for evening count. Night calls are hit and miss and, of course, those are my favorite because I like his voice to be the last one I hear before I go to sleep. Sometimes, on really rare occasions, he can squeeze a call in before work in the morning – and that's usually right when I'm pulling into my own job. It's a great way to start the day and I wish those calls happened more often, too.

Recently, someone very close to him was found to have terminal cancer. She wasn't given very long to live at all and because I'm the only person who is in constant contact with him, I had to tell him. It was one of the hardest things I've ever done. I also called the chaplain at the prison to ask permission for Mark to call and speak to her. They allowed him to call – but only for 60 seconds. All I could think was, how could one human say to another human, "I know how much this person means to you and this could be the last time you ever speak to them, but you have one minute" - a chaplain, nonetheless! Thankfully, she was sent home from the hospital on hospice, and he did get to talk to her just one more time. She passed on his 34th birthday, which was also a day that I visited, and I felt his grief in my soul. It kept me up at night knowing that he was hurting and was in there with no outlet. Can you imagine losing a person that you love and look up to in every way and not being able to say goodbye face to face, and then having to grieve when constantly surrounded by hundreds of other people who expect you to have no emotion? Just imagine what that's like.

I also handle some legal issues for him because he is unable to do it on his own from prison, though these things are expected to be completed by parole to get a good review and approval. The system is, in many ways, set up for inmates to fail, and without someone who cares for them and will help them, a lot of them do.

Some of the things I've dealt with include attempting to get his property back from the police department that arrested him and held his things for evidence. I've also been trying to take care of all the requirements on his driver's license suspension so that his license can be reinstated upon his release since he will be paroling to my home. Since I live in a rural area, personal transportation is a must.

Though parole is still several years away for us, I still spend a good deal of time worrying about it. The last thing I want, after 12 years of his life has been wasted behind bars, is for him to have to do more time. There is no such thing as pre-release or "good time" where we live, so the earliest he will be released is his minimum date. I hope every single day that it all goes as planned, and he can come home to me at the first opportunity.

I did worry for a while that he wasn't "done" getting in trouble yet. I asked myself often, what if I wait for this man, and he comes home and goes right back? I didn't really talk to him about that concern, but it's almost like he knew what was on my mind. He wrote me a letter and told me that he is retiring from his "criminal career" and that he never wants to do anything that will take him away from me again. He is 34 years old. He has missed so much including his children growing up. Deep in my heart, I believe that he's being genuine. Some people say those are just words and that it's all in the actions. They're right, but it still soothes my heart to know that this was on his mind as well as mine.

People often ask me how I do it or seem surprised when I tell them that my fiancé is in prison. I don't keep it a secret because he's a part of me and his story is a part of mine. I live day to day, one day at a time. I count to small milestones – like "2 more months until my birthday" or "2 weeks until the 4th of July". We get as much contact as we can so we can stay close as possible. I involve him in my life by asking his opinion on decisions I need to make and actually taking them into account because I value his input – even down to simple things like "do you think I should color my hair black or red?"

There is nothing fun about being in prison or being a prison wife, but there are ways to make it bearable. I've also found companionship and understanding in other prison wives – those I've met online and those I've met at Mark's facility. Reaching out to people who understand is so important to this journey for me. I feel compelled to talk about Mark so much that it probably annoys people but not my prison wife friends. They understand, they listen, and they relate and it's wonderful not to have to censor myself for them.

Mark has many skills in many different trades from doing construction to working as a chef to roofing, plumbing, or HVAC and much more. Upon his release, though, he hopes to get back into doing auto body work, and he hopes to eventually run his own garage. He enjoys working on cars and even does so in his free time when he's home. He also loves to fish and hunt and is dedicated to learning to hunt with a crossbow, because as a felon, he can no longer own a firearm. He is a country boy at heart and we have decided that, once he is off parole, we would like to move to Tennessee – close to Nashville – because we are both lovers of music and, where better to enjoy it than Music City?

I tell you these things because it's important to remember that behind every DOC number, behind every inmate, there is a story to be told. There is a person just like you and me who just happened to make a mistake that cost him or her years of their life. Not every person in prison is a bad person, just like not every person out here walking the streets is a good one.

Though I can't wait until this is all a distant memory when Mark is free and we are living our life together out here, I have learned valuable lessons about life, my relationship, and myself on this journey that I will always hold onto. For that, I am thankful.

Just have lots of love and patience. - Jody

Leah

God gives his hardest battles to his strongest soldiers. - Arce

I met my husband when I was just out of high school. Although we dated for a little while, our lives took us in different directions. We both married other people and had other children. We did remain friends during that time, but when those relationships ended in divorce, we decided that we were meant to be together.

Brian had been incarcerated before we met. It wasn't anything I was accustomed to, but I overlooked it because I cared about him. When he started to get into trouble and eventually was charged with a parole violation, I felt like I didn't have a right to complain or be upset about it. He had been in trouble before. I knew that about him. I accepted that part of him when I decided to be in a relationship with him, so I felt like I should just understand that this was a part of who he was.

Through the course of five or six years, I spent so much time hiding from other people how I felt. I didn't feel like I could share my emotions about Brian being incarcerated with them. I didn't feel like I was entitled to them because it isn't like I didn't know about his past. I felt like I should've known that this was a possibility for our lives together. When other people didn't know what was going on with Brian, I might say he was out of town. I left a majority of people uninformed about Brian being in prison.

I felt like a single mother. All outsiders assumed that I was a single mother. It wasn't that I ever went out partying or talked to other guys. It was just that I felt like I was all alone in dealing with the responsibilities in my daily life because he wasn't physically there. I couldn't get over feeling like he chose not to be there with me.

I felt an overwhelming amount of pain. I felt that he had made choices that caused our little family to suffer. In fact, my husband made choices that caused him to miss the birth of our third and fifth children completely. He was incarcerated when our fourth came as well, but he was given a family furlough to attend that birth. He had to turn himself in a few hours after our baby girl was born. It was so hurtful knowing that while I had been sitting at home, carrying our children, being a mother to my other children, being a wife to him; he decided to do things that caused him to get into trouble. I felt like he let that happen without considering me or our children at all. I wholeheartedly blamed him.

I was also embarrassed that my husband, a part of MY FAMILY, was in prison. In the small town in Arkansas that I was from, that wasn't a common thing. I didn't know anyone that had been to jail or prison with the exception of this man I had married. There was a very short list of individuals I spoke with about Brian and no one I knew personally was on that list.

I did find solace in an online network of prison wives, girlfriends, fiancés, and families. It was that group of women who were pulled together through this unfortunate set of circumstances that helped me to come to terms with the life that my family was shoved into. Each day I logged into The Visiting Room to see what was going on with my online contacts. At the time, it was a fairly small group of women from across the United States and other countries. I had never met them, but I felt like I'd known them for years. I related to them. I understood what they were saying, and I felt what they were feeling.

In considering what these ladies were saying, I realized that it was okay to express how I felt. It was okay to let outsiders know that I was hurt and angry. I was lonely. I was disappointed in this person that had pledged his life to me and finally, I felt like it was okay to say it. Maybe I did marry this person knowing that he had been in trouble, but darn it, I didn't have to accept that it was just the way my life was going to be or that there couldn't be more to our life together.

Even though I loved Brian dearly, I was pretty frustrated at him for getting into trouble. When I finally believed that it was acceptable to express the way that I felt, I was able to be more open and honest with Brian about my emotional well-being and how I felt about his incarceration than I'd ever been before. I was always honest about things that occurred, but being open with my feelings about Brian's incarceration worked to bring us closer as a couple. I felt like I could accept his flaws and love him as much as I did while also admitting to myself that he had screwed up most any good thing that we had at the time.

Being angry didn't mean that I wasn't going to be supportive of him. I was supportive. Every single day I was supportive. I did what I could do to be there for my husband while he was away. I understood that prison wasn't easy. That isn't to say that I knew everything about prison life. I definitely didn't, and I didn't want to know the details. It wasn't for me to know some things. I just wanted my husband and me to get past it so that he could come back home safely.

The anger also didn't mean that I didn't depend on Brian or lean on him to some extent. I did rely on him. He was still my husband. He was still my children's father. If I needed to talk to someone about something, he was that one. If I had concerns, issues, whatever, I took them all to him. That bond wasn't broken when he didn't live up to society's expectations. For better or worse, we were together.

A really great thing about Brian was that he didn't reject the way I was feeling. My husband comforted me by telling me that it wasn't my fault. He did take some responsibility for what had happened. Once we were really over being open about how we both felt over what happened we were able to work to overcome more issues and have better communication.

One thing that really helped us was to rely on God, the Bible, and our religion. I read a really good illustration once about marriage and your relationship with God. It said to imagine yourself on one side of a hill and your spouse on the other. God was at the top. The more you strive to become closer to your God, the higher you go up the hill. If you and your mate are both moving in the direction of God, you're also becoming closer to each other. Since we are both religious people, it helped us to envision this. It wasn't that we would ever be at the perfect place. Clearly, ours was a marriage marked with imperfection. We may not have been in a great place all of the time, but if we are both working toward the same goal, we are both growing toward each other.

There were so many other issues that we had to figure out and work through during his incarceration. Child rearing from a distance, how to approach all circumstances, how we dealt with unsupportive people, how we faced the loss of jobs, homes, and income, as well as generalized relationship and trust issues that any marriage might face.

When it came to how to approach issues that faced me and our family on the outside, I had only seen how Brian's mother had dealt with things. Angie, Brian's mom, had a strict policy not to tell him anything that could cause him more stress. She hid things from him, and she had everyone else hide things from him. I don't think that she saw herself as being deceitful. I think that she felt that it was what she had to do in order to protect him, and that worked for her. It worked for everyone else as well. It worked until the day that I was forced to make a heart-wrenching phone call to the chaplain at the prison.

In 2006, Brian and I were dating, although we hadn't really told anyone yet. I was a single mom of a little boy. At the time, I was a full-time employee at the local hospital. I enjoyed my job until that day. I saw Brian's dad, Keith, and his brother, Dennis, walk through the door of the emergency room looking panicked. I had been busy back in the emergency room, so I didn't really pay much attention to it. We had a 54-year-old Jane Doe coming in by EMS, and it didn't look good. She hadn't made it there yet, but after I saw Keith and Dennis, I quickly connected the dots. Angie was 54. My heart sank as I let the ER staff know that Jane Doe's name was Angie, and her family was waiting. I didn't say anything to Dennis or Keith. It wasn't my place. A few minutes later, I saw Brian's other brother and sister in law, Chase and Sophia, come in through the door.

I was there when they brought Angie in. I saw them transfer her to a gurney and frantically try to save her. They announced her time of death but hadn't told the family yet. I was told to have them move to the chapel. I did, and that was when Chase cornered me and demanded to know what I knew. I knew that I couldn't tell him. I would've lost my job, but I also felt so bad about not telling him. It wasn't the worst that I was going to feel, though.

The worst part came before they left the hospital when they said that I could tell Brian if I wanted to, but they weren't going to. 'What? Why? Why wouldn't you tell him?' I asked. I didn't really receive any kind of response. So, I did call the prison. I called the prison and asked to speak with the chaplain. The chaplain asked for the details. What happened? What hospital? Where's the hospital located? What was the cause of death? What time did she die? Where could they reach me? Did I know when the service would be? I answered all of the questions that I could, and I waited for Brian to call back.

It seemed like I waited quite a while before Brian called again. All these years have passed, and I can still hear his stoic voice say those words. They were really the only words that he had to say until they were answered. "What happened?" Brian would've been upset anyway because he and his mother were so close, but you see, she didn't tell him about her health issues. The ones that he knew about, she had told him they weren't a big deal. Angie died of a massive heart attack, and I still believe that a piece of Brian died too.

It was from that experience that I learned not to hide things from him. Yes, the things that I've had to say over the years have stressed him out. Yes, it's been hard to tell him some of the things

I've had to say because I knew it would be upsetting, but I did it because I had a firsthand knowledge of what the alternative could be.

One of the other things that we had to overcome was figuring out how to raise children in this circumstance. That was another very difficult thing. We haven't always had similar views on things that should be included in a child's life, but we did always agree on one thing for sure: a father should always play a role in their child's life. Brian spent time writing letters to the kids, and they drew pictures to send back to him. He would call them a couple of times a week to talk to them, and see how their week was going. The older we got, when we went to visitation, it became less about us as a couple and more about our family and the children spending time with daddy.

When they met milestones, I made sure to encourage them to share it with their father. When we took pictures, I always let them pick out one to send to dad. I did what I could to keep him playing an active father role. I always made sure to tell the kids that mommy and daddy both loved them. He did love them, and I knew that they needed to know that.

Two things about it were difficult for me. We didn't always agree on how to discipline the children when they'd done something that they weren't supposed to. The other thing was that it was difficult for me to explain to them where daddy was when they were younger. In time, Brian did trust my judgment when it came to discipline, because I was there in the situation, and he wasn't. It wasn't that he never had input on what to do. He did have a say. He could tell me how he felt, or what he would do, but ultimately he left it up to me. I showed my appreciation for that by letting him know how things went. Another thing he did that really did help the situation was to have my back. He would write letters to the kids discussing with them what had happened, and really let them know to 'listen to mommy'. It did help me so much that he did that. It meant that the kids knew that we united in raising them.

I'll be honest. I hated the kids asking where daddy was. It wasn't that I didn't want for them to know, but how can you explain that to a three-year-old? I did always try to be honest with them and give them age appropriate information. A three-year-old is generally familiar with time out. I told the kids that daddy had done something that was a no-no, and he was in a long time out because look how many years old he was. I let them know that daddy would be back home after they let him out of time out, but he had to wait for now. I did always put it on daddy. I didn't want for the kids to think that it was something that was done to daddy. I wanted for the children to feel a certain respect for taking responsibility for your actions. I made it as clear as I could that this was something that daddy did.

I know that it really isn't a popular thing to say "yes I did it" in prison, but I did feel like if there was ever a chance that the kids were going to be different, victimizing a person being sent to prison for their actions wasn't the way to go. That being said, I do realize that there are people that are incarcerated for crimes that they didn't commit. It was just that Brian wasn't one of those people, and I wasn't going to make it sound like he was.

Through the years, we have had to deal with more than our fair share of unsupportive people. It wasn't just his incarceration that was a problem. It was our relationship as a whole. Neither his family nor my family was ever really supportive of us. His family saw the changes that he made after we were married, and felt like he was a different person. My family felt like I changed because they saw me as being more accepting of things that I wasn't raised to tolerate.

Given the chance, any one of them would've tried to put doubt in the other one. In fact, that's exactly what happened. His family would write him, and tell him that I had made friends that I hadn't, that I was doing things I wasn't, or that I said things I didn't. The goal was to make him think that I was moving forward with my life without him.

My family was constantly talking to me about how I deserved better (not that I didn't want my husband to be better), how he had other people writing him, that he was probably in a relationship with some other man in prison because "that's what felons do", or even how he wouldn't be any different or make any changes when he came home. It was all to sow seeds of doubt.

Brian let his family quickly know that the changes were a result of his own choices because he had grown tired of the way he was living. He also made it clear that we told each other everything, so he knew exactly what I was doing and what I wasn't doing. I told my family that Brian was my husband, and I was his wife. We didn't get married just to turn around and get divorced, and if we would figure things out together. We had to become our own team.

We also had to overcome financial issues. During one time when Brian was locked up, I lost a good job that I had. I didn't have much money for phone calls or visitation anymore. I couldn't send Brian as much money as I did before. Some people might wonder how this was a hardship that our relationship faced and not just a difficult situation that I faced alone. The answer is this: when you're a team, everything that happens to one affects the other.

When I didn't have money to talk to Brian, we worried ourselves sick about each other. We lived in a state where the price of a phone call was ridiculously expensive, and I never lived close to where a prison was, so we mostly relied on letters and emails. I also wanted to talk to him every day. The way his voice made everything okay was just what I needed. There was a time that I spoke with him every day, sometimes multiple times a day, but phone calls from him were expensive, and it ended up being a significant amount of money. I had spent up to $75 a day on phone calls before but after a couple of children that also wasn't an option. At the time, the calls from jail were $25 for two fifteen minute calls. Even though the calls from prison were a little cheaper, I could still only get two and a half calls for $25.

What I chose to do most of the time was email. I could email him through a program called Access Corrections, the prison would print it out and deliver it to him at mail call, and he would write me back a letter to respond. The best thing about being able to send emails was that if I sent it before midnight, he would get it the next day. It wasn't as fast as a phone call, but it was faster than snail mail.

One of the more difficult things for Brian about me not having money was that he didn't get commissary like he had before. I simply couldn't send him money like he was accustomed to. There were some months that I didn't get to send him anything at all. It wasn't until I found a new job and started working full time again that I was able to send money to help support him like I had before. He was upset at the situation. That's understandable. The Department of Corrections only gave them enough to survive, which left Brian hungry even after eating a meal, so not having food to supplement made it more difficult for him.

He said something to me about it that let me know that it was all going to be okay. He told me that he would be fine. He said 'Take care of yourself and the kids. Send me money when you can. I'll be alright.' I did send money as soon as I could because I knew that he was borrowing and owed people, but I appreciated his attitude as well. He could've just been sitting in his bunk thinking about himself and his hunger, but he was thinking about me and the children instead.

When I had to write letters through the mail, it took letters two to three days each way. That meant to complete correspondence about one little thing, it took at least 6 days. Much of the time, I had to take into consideration that the prison didn't have incoming or outgoing mail on Saturday. If I sent a letter after Wednesday, he definitely wouldn't receive it until Monday.

While I would've loved the opportunity to see my love every weekend, it just wasn't a possibility. Even with the perfect circumstances of having money and a vehicle, it was a difficult trip.

We just didn't get to go that much. I tried to find others to ride with, but a majority of people going to visitation often were living in the vicinity of the prison. I couldn't find anyone that I could trust and feel safe with that was coming from anywhere near my area. Sometimes I only got to go to visitation once every few months.

It was difficult that during that time Brian didn't get to watch the kids grow up like he would've wanted to. I remember in 2013-2014, we only got to go to visitation twice in that year. I tried to send more pictures of the kids so that he could see the kids, but it was hard for everyone. Of course, the kids wanted to go see their daddy. Not having visitation to spend physical time together made the time drag by so much slower. It also made the kids miss him even more.

I was always someone that craved affection. It wasn't just that I enjoyed it. It was that I felt like I needed it in order to feel loved. When Brian was in prison, I had to learn to live without feeling his touch, and it wasn't easy for me. It wasn't the sex. I could live without that easily. It was having the person that I loved so dearly not being home to hug me every day or having them to hold my hand when we prayed. I wanted to be kissed. I needed to be held in his arms.

During the course of our marriage, Brian and I had been very loving toward each other. Even if it was something as simple as watching a movie on the couch with my head on his shoulder, it was the little things that we shared before he went to jail that I loved and enjoyed. Each time he went back to prison, I felt like those things were taken away from me and it was difficult.

It took time for me to grow accustomed to the lack of intimacy each time. For years, even when he wasn't home I would sleep on my side of the bed away from the door. I left his side untouched for him. His pillow stayed in its place. I went to bed at night feeling incredibly lonely. I longed for his touch. When I woke up in the morning, it felt like I always had a secret hope that he would be home. I imagined that he would somehow be released and show up at home to surprise me. I always felt disappointed that he was never there.

When I would do things with the children throughout the day, I would wonder what he would say about it or what he would think of it. With so many of the things that happened I tried to consider what it would be like if Brian were there. If something funny came up, I would think "Brian would laugh so hard. I need to tell him that." I felt like he was an active part of our lives even when he was gone.

It did help for me to allow Brian to be an active part of our lives. It wasn't just for him. It helped me to allow him to take on the roles of being a father and being a husband when he came home. It let the kids adjust faster to his return. In my opinion, it made the situation better for all of us.

Even though we had so many difficult things to overcome, we did come out of it with our heads held high. In 2016, Brian flattened his sentence. I couldn't be happier that we don't have prison or parole hanging over our heads. The first 17 years that I knew Brian were tough, but I learned that it's possible to get past all of it.

Don't ever give up! It's hard, a struggle every day. My husband has a very long sentence, but we aren't giving up on bringing him home sooner. Surround yourself with positive people. — Tracy

Insights and Viewpoints

It's a struggle but I love my husband more than anything, and I believe in him.

- Holly

I became an admin for the support group that I enjoyed in 2014. Through that, I learn about so many women who are in the same situation I was in. They don't know what to do or how they are going to make it through. It can honestly be so overwhelming to imagine yourself writing letters to someone in prison and waiting for the day that they'll come home knowing it will be years down the road.

I don't have much wisdom to offer on the subject. Really all I know is what I've seen and what I've experienced. One thing that I do know for sure is that if you go into this half hearted or uncertain that you want to do it, it will be harder for you to stick it through. Those who aren't sure that they want to stick around almost always end up leaving.

So many prison families will say that this life isn't for everyone. That's true. I have been the one to meet all of my children's day to day needs for all of these years. I had to fill in all of the gaps that Brian left. I probably could've found someone to fill that space and take on that role. I didn't because that wasn't the right thing for me to do. Sometimes for some people, the pressure of taking everything on alone is too much. For other people, they can't live without the affection that comes with having a mate at home. Having a mate in prison isn't an easy thing to do at all. It's night after night of crying and loneliness. It's sometimes finding solace in inanimate objects that meant nothing before.

No one should tell another person the right or wrong way to have a mate in prison or jail because it's different for everyone. It's similar to having a relationship on the outside in that way. Everyone's relationship, charge, and time are all different. The units are different. The states are different. There's a pretty significant difference in having a mate in federal prison versus having one in state prison. There's a whole world of difference between having someone in county jail and having someone in state Department of Corrections.

A lot of times people start to feel lonely. I know I did. My circumstances changed along the time that Brian was gone. Then they changed again. Sometimes I felt so lonely, and sometimes I didn't feel it as much. When I got lonely, I got depressed. I think that's something that a number of prison wives or families face. Loneliness or general sadness and depression go together for some people. It's important to keep yourself occupied and not to be sucked in by the difficult time that you face. Write some letters. Write a story together. Do a workbook with your mate or complete a couple's program. Find activities to do outside of the prison and your loved one's incarceration. Finding new hobbies or interests isn't just something that can occupy your time; it's also something new that you can talk to your loved one about.

While I felt a wide variety of emotions during the time that my husband was gone, I knew that I was going to stick around and try to keep my family intact. I felt that I had made a commitment when I married this person, so I knew that rain or shine, in good times and bad, I was going to be there for him. It certainly wasn't easy, but it was the right decision for me. I remember so many days that were difficult. It felt as though I was struggling through my day just waiting for my phone to ring so that I could completely unload all of my worries and cares on the person on the other end. When you're in that situation, I think that it's important to accept and legitimize all of the many emotions that you feel. Maybe not every person that has a loved one in prison feels a certain way, but it can be assured that you aren't the only person that's ever felt that way. Your commitment absolutely has to be bigger than the difficulty that your mate's sentence causes. You have to be stronger than your situation.

If you allow it to, having an incarcerated loved one will destroy you. Other people having input in your life and in your relationship will make you second guess everything that you thought you knew about the person that you're waiting for. Don't let others sow seeds of doubt in your relationship. Some will say things that you never thought that they would. You will hear all sorts of stories about relationships that didn't work out. You are the best judge of your relationship. Know that things do happen. There are men (and women) behind bars that will use you to their satisfaction, and then leave you behind when they are released. This can happen whether you met while the other was incarcerated or not. I had no guarantee that my mate would return to me, but I did have enough faith that I knew the person that he was.

People will try to tell you that you're doing the wrong thing by being there for a criminal. That's something that isn't for anyone else to decide. That's something that is for you alone to figure out. If you feel like it's not for you to be with someone that's in prison then walk away now. Don't wait until you get invested in things or make yourself or that other person think that you're going to be there. If what you decide is that this is something that you can do and want to do, then dig in your heels. There will always be someone that disapproves. You just have to have your mind set enough that it doesn't matter what anyone thinks or says.

Don't feel guilty in the moments that you enjoy. Don't laugh, but then feel like you shouldn't get to have a good time because your mate is in a DOC unit somewhere. You can laugh, enjoy things, and love life even with your mate being locked up. Loving life or enjoying yourself doesn't mean that you love your partner any less. It can help you to be a better, happier, more upbeat person for them. Life does go on past incarceration.

It's important to be open and honest with your loved one. They don't know what happens on the outside unless someone tells them. Keeping things from your loved one can cause confusion. It can make room for other people to come between you and your mate by them telling your loved one things before you decide to tell them. If you are open with each other, you have the opportunity to work through things as they come. You will have an important and powerful trust between you.

I am of the opinion that supporting your mate during their time does not mean that you support their crime. Let me say that again because this is something that many outsiders lack understanding with. SUPPORTING YOUR MATE THROUGH THEIR CRIME DOES NOT MEAN THAT YOU SUPPORT THEIR CRIME. There are no victimless crimes. Some charges are more serious in nature, but they all have victims somewhere. I chose to accept my spouse in spite of his criminal background. I don't love that about him, but I do love him regardless of it.

However you feel, please know that it takes a strong individual to maintain any long distance relationship for very long. If you are doing this with your mate, know that you're an extraordinary kind of being. So many women find it difficult to go very long without spending time with their loved one. A person that's committing themselves to a relationship with someone that has time to serve is accepting that they won't have that intimacy with their mate for a certain length of time. Sharing life with an inmate is lonesome. There are no bedtime cuddles to be had. There's no alone time unless you're in one of the few states that still have family (conjugal) visits. If your mate is approved for contact visits, you still aren't getting a hug or kiss without someone watching practically every move. There isn't a phone call that happens or mail that's sent or received without the prospect of someone knowing exactly what you're saying.

If you can handle those things, you should know that you are unique from many people in society. In some ways, you are more independent and maybe even stronger. Your life on the outside probably won't meet the standards of the individuals around you, but it will be your life with your incarcerated loved one.

Quotes and Other Words

of Advice

I asked a group of ladies that were supporting their incarcerated loved ones a few questions. These were their responses.

What piece of advice would you give to other people that are supporting their incarcerated loved ones?

Today is one step closer than yesterday. — *Anonymous*

Stay positive. Each day that goes by, you're a step closer to having your loved one. — *Jade*

To stay strong and remember every day down is another day closer to their loved one coming home. — *Rachel*

Pray every day. — *Na'ilah*

Be committed, be faithful, and always let them know what's going on. My husband's family used to tell me not to tell him anything negative that went on within the family. They wanted to protect him and not make him stress. My husband told me to tell him everything. The worst thing besides cheating that you can do is to make them feel out of sight out of mind. — Emily

Be supportive & have faith. — Ruby

Life is tough but knowing you have someone waiting makes it worthwhile. — Cindy

Love and Pray. — Alicia

Love will conquer all. — Malinda

Take 1 day at a time that's what got me thru all the madness of an incarcerated loved one. — Marlene

Get a hobby. You will worry yourself crazy! — Nicole

Be Strong For Both You & Your Loved One That Is Incarcerated & Never Leave Their Side. — Melissa

Have a support group!! — Vicki

Don't give up! Sometimes it gets you down always doing things alone but it's ten times worse for them! Know that you are the sunshine in their world and just always try to encourage them! — Shawna

Be patient and understanding. Things happen that are out of their control. — Shannon

Try not to argue over trivial things. Choose your battles. He's your teammate, not your opponent. — Anonymous

Be patient. — Monica

This is hard but be strong. — Lorena

Just have faith and patience. — Tara

Don't listen to the negative feedback from people who do not agree with you standing by your loved one's side. Tough skin is a must in this ride. — Pschigoda

Don't ever give up. It's hard and there will be ups and downs, but it's all worth it. — Anonymous

Don't judge them and be there for one another. — Anonymous

Have patience. — Robin

Always write letters. — Anonymous

Stay busy. It makes the time go by faster. — Jami

Be Strong For Both You & Your Loved One That Is Incarcerated & Never Leave Their Side. — Melissa

Take it day by day.

Always keep yourself busy.

Communication is key. — Anonymous

You need to have a lot of patience. — Jen

Support your loved one, means everything to them. — Denise

Write everything down. — Stevie

Stay strong. – Dawna

Be patient. Life inside the walls is backward than our life. He once said "what is supposed to be isn't. What isn't supposed to be is." Also, love hard, write as often as possible. It helps both y'all more than either one of you could ever imagine. – Stacey

Watch for red flags. If something is too good to be true it is. If they are asking for money and become angry if you can't that is a problem. – Kim

Honesty is so important. – Stephanie

Be patient and supportive. Have as much communication as possible. – Ashley

Make sure that you take time to care for yourself. – Janette

There will be bad days. Stay strong. – Anonymous

Use this as a time to make you stronger. Let go of the idea of your former life, and start looking forward. Find new dreams, and just keep going. – Michelle

Do what makes you happy and don't listen to other people. – Brittany

They rely on you to be their voice while incarcerated. – Misty

Be patient. – Anonymous

Stay strong. – Yvette

Try your best! – Vanessa

Keep it in the moment, don't look at incarceration time. Staying connected is very important, do things together even though you are separated, watch TV programs, listen to the radio, watch sports, read the same books all at the same time, have the time together. Try to make the best of the not so best situation and talk, share thoughts and feelings. – Anonymous

Stay strong and be ready for anything. – Stacy

Love letters really are jail talk. Never marry someone u MWI before u see them and how they are in the streets. – Rikki

Say what you mean, and mean what you say. – Jasmine

Be patient. – Rhonda

Be there for them. – Rhonda

Communication is key, and you HAVE to also take care of yourself. –Kristen

Never give up hope or listen to these people when they say you should because that's what they want. It makes their job easier. – Danny

Don't give up. They need you as much as you need them. – Teresa

Don't allow the worry to consume you. – Irma

Never give up on yourself or your loved one. They are counting on you. – Kayla

Patience and communication are key. – Brittany

Never give up on them even when times are hard. They need are love and support. We are the only piece of the outside world that they have left. They need to know they are loved and not just a number to the system. – Heather

Write to them as often as possible, almost as if you are journaling. It's therapeutic for you as well as let's your incarcerated loved one know how things are going day to day. – Anonymous

Care for yourself first. — Julie

Don't go at it half assed. —Betty

Stay strong! — Summer

Have lots of patience. — Jody

Just keep moving forward and take one day at a time. — Belinda

Communication is important. — Maria

To keep you focused on what is to be honest and keep your head up. — Holly

Always keep your head held high. — Laura

Be strong, stay strong, and trust in God. — Anonymous

Stay strong. The wait doesn't last forever. — Trina

Stand by their side no matter what! The good, bad & everything in between. — Anonymous

Don't give up on him. It will be worth it in the end. — Beth

Support assists in better rehabilitation, encouragement, aides in change when one is down and feels like giving up one's strength and support is meaningful. — Queena

Stay connected to God only him can guide you and get you through this. — Elisa

Be prepared for a roller coaster and know you may be their only outlet. — Marie

Take it one day at a time, make sure to have a good life on the outside so you stay sane. Take care of yourself so you can be there when they need you. — Anonymous

Never let the attitude of the incarcerated get you down. Sometimes you are the only one they can let their frustrations out on. — Stephanie

Stay busy!! Work, kids (if you have them) or some other activity or hobbies. — Mandy

Be positive and encourage them. – Lona

Have God in your life. He will guide you through it all. – Arce

Don't forget the positive. Support progress of rehab. Visit as much as possible. Don't beat yourself up for things out of your control. – Deena

Hang in there. Stay strong. – Anonymous

Patience – Veronica

Stay strong. – Rosalia

Don't give up!!! Keep communication of all forms going: Phone calls, visits, letters. Try to make friends in similar situations, and stay around the family that supports you during this time. – Tracy

Be patient. Give them lots of love. They need it now the most. – Delores

Stay strong. – Tiesha

Don't put your life on hold. – P

Be patient. – Kourtney

Do your very best to keep a positive perception on this journey. Keep your head held high, and keep on loving your significant other! – Jenn

Make sure before you take on this huge commitment, that you truly, truly love the person. It gets so difficult but the love that you have for each other makes it bearable enough to hang in there and be strong when things seem impossible or when you feel you just can't physically or mentally do it. – Alexis

Never give up. – Brandi

There will be lots of ups and downs. Remain who you are and stay true to yourself first and then you can be there for your loved one. – Krista

Never lie to them. – Cindy

Pray to never give up hope and strength for your loved one! – Katie

Stay strong and remember why you are waiting. ❤ *- Bo*

Be patient, supportive and understanding. – Patches

Have lots of patience and show a lot of love and support! – Carmen

Be honest & send lots of letters & pictures. – Izzy

Be patient love them through their manic episodes. Pray for your men daily. – Katie

Keep the lines of communication open at all times. – Anonymous

Have patience. Know what's being said, what's being heard and what's being understood! – LaToya

What do you wish you'd known before that you know now?

Being married or in a relationship with someone incarcerated is not an easy task you have to stand strong and be supportive in so many ways. Also being with one isn't just about being in love, letters, and visits. It's about reassuring that rehabilitation is set forward, classes, counseling, etc is being giving to ensure this love one reenters society in a positive way so recidivism doesn't play a part in ones future. It's not easy, but when you love someone, you will fight for them to be better. — Queena

It's hard, but it's absolutely worth the wait! — Patches

Be prepared for judgment. — LaToya

It's a hard ride but love, prayer, and hope will help you get through. – Katie

Honestly I wouldn't recommend it. This isn't something I went seeking. It's a big challenge. Make sure you are up for it before you get into it (if you can). – Anonymous

I stand by loved ones side because I want to not because I have to. – Pschigoda

It's scary, but it gets easier. – Jade

No one can really understand your situation because every case is different just keep an open mind and be there for each other. – Cindy

It isn't easy, it takes commitment. If you are someone who can't be be alone for a long period of time it is not the life for you. — Emily

It's hard. You can't feel sorry for yourself if you chose this life. — Nicole

It's hard but if you love someone you love them and that means no matter what! — Shawna

I'm married to a wonderful man. Just because he's locked up doesn't mean I will turn my back on him. We'll get thru this together. — Denise

Be understanding; try to put yourself in their shoes. And try to always end the phone call on a good note. You never know when you will talk to them again. Do to lock down, moved to a new location or phones going down. — Jami

It's hard and sometimes you feel like giving up but if the love is real, it's worth it. — Anonymous

There are a lot of sacrifices in this lifestyle, you have to have patience. It's not an easy road. — Robin

It's hard but it gets manageable. — Marlene

However hard things seem for you, you have to remember that it's always a little harder for them and that you HAVE to stay strong and somewhat positive for them and their wellbeing because it's easier for them in there to lose it. — Alexis

It's a complicated, anxiety inducing, life changing event that happens to you and your family. The pain of incarceration isn't placed on only the incarcerated individuals; and yes, they are INDIVIDUALS. It doesn't matter their location. They are still human beings and deserve to be treated as such. — Irma

Don't waste your stamps or paid phone calls on petty fighting. Continue to encourage your loved one to work on bettering themselves. Keep busy and better yourself as well. Learn to be patient. For example, just because he says he'll call at a certain time, doesn't mean he 100% can. Things happen. It's prison and none of us, inside or out, have any control over things like that. Remember, it's not just you who's upset ... YOUR SIGNIFICANT OTHER MISSES YOU TOO. — Brittany

It's hard sometimes because the system is trying everything they can to keep us apart. They don't like that I met him while I worked there. Then they don't like that we are a black and white couple. I love my boyfriend, and I don't see what they see. He is more than just an inmate he is a man who made a wrong choice. Why not let him serve his time in peace he has long enough as is? Why make it harder on him? They want to take our visits so that way we can't see each other and that will break us. We have to be at the mercy of the warden to get them back. How can people sleep at night knowing this hurts people? – Heather

It's never easy and it's always expensive. But no matter what visits are mandatory. It doesn't matter the distance or the cost. If you care you will find a way. – Rikki

Be understanding, try to put yourself in their shoes, and try to always end the phone call on a good note. You never know when you will talk to them again due to lock down, being moved to a new location or phones going down. – Jami

116

What helps you make it through?

Pictures, letters, and drawings! – Rachel

Communication - Na'ilah

I know I will have my husband home one day. That gives me hope and faith. –
Emily

My Love for him & knowing that one day he will be home. – Ruby

Knowing that my love for him can overcome anything that comes our way. –
Cindy

Prayer – Alicia

Knowing that one day he will be home. – Malinda

Cry it out and praying. – Marlene

Emails from my boyfriend and music. – Nicole

Reading old letters and reminiscing our moments together. – Melissa W

When he calls me! – Vicki

Getting to video visit makes it a lot better they can see home and their families a lot easier and it makes those bad days. — Shawna

The knowledge that he loves me, and we will be together again. — Shannon

Phone calls — Anonymous

Praying — Monica

Being able to talk to him and knowing that we can visit on weekends. — Tara

Knowing there is hope now. We can now see the light at the end of the tunnel with all these new laws. — Lorena

119

Knowing that I'm doing what my heart feels is right. — Pschigoda

All I do is look up and pray to God. I even just look to the sky and say we got another day down. — Anonymous

His emails make my entire day just knowing what he is doing in there. — Anonymous

That phone call — Robin

Rereading letters. — Anonymous

Read or anything to keep your mind off of the situation. — Jami

Continue to live your life, and include your loved one as much as you can in every decision. – Jen

God, and knowing each passing day is a day closer. Focus on situations on the outside. – Denise

My children and family support. – Anonymous

My work – Shawna

All I do is look up and pray to God. I even just look to the sky and say we got another day down. – Anonymous

Writing to him. – Izzy

Reminding myself that he misses me as much as I miss him. — Katie

To remember that this is only temporary, and he will be home soon. — Bo

His picture, prayer, thinking about a future with him. — Katie

Writing to him gets me through the difficult days. I tell him how I'm feeling and it makes me feel closer to him. — Patches

Picturing his face — Cindy

Praying — Mandy

Keeping hobbies or activities that I enjoy. It's a good distraction. – Krista

Just remembering the amazing moments that we had together as a family. – Jenn

Focusing on the bright future that my loved one and I talk/dream so much about. – Alexis

Don't let other peoples opinion matter in your relationship pretty much don't tell your business to others that will not understand your situation – Arce

Daydreaming about the future. Making plans or keeping a running bucket list. Looking forward to the smaller countdowns, the next letter and the next visit. – Mandy

Exercise, distractions, family outings, looking at pics or rereading a letter if I'm really missing him. – Anonymous

Rereading letters, waiting for the next phone call or visit & more than anything knowing he's coming home one day. – Anonymous

Our love is one of a kind. Knowing and remembering all we have been through keeps me strong on this difficult journey. – Summer

Facebook groups – Holly

Reading letters – Maria

Talking to him on the phone – Belinda

Being able to hear his voice — Trina

Remembering that it's not forever — Julie

Getting it out on paper — Anonymous

I have faith because without that I have nothing. — Beth

Faith and meditation — Marie

Faith in God — Elisa

Knowing that he is going to be there for me as soon as he can (not physically but emotionally). – Kayla

The thought that one day it will be over – Kristen

His voice and self care. I love mani/pedi's – Rhonda

Our daughter – Jasmine

Hope life will get better – Rikki

To let go of the should-haves, and could haves. To accept this situation for what it is, and understand there is a plan that is bigger than me. Also to lay on the couch and watch movies – Michelle

126

Writing in my journal – Janette

Staying busy – Brittany

Talk to the girls in my prison wife group and talking to my husband –
Anonymous

A couple specific support groups, reading old letters, listening to recordings of
our phone calls that I have and most importantly keeping myself busy. –
Brittany

I know my boyfriend loves me and when days are really hard, like right now he
is in confinement for something he did not do, so there are no phone calls home,
and they have taken our visits for god knows how long, but I reread old letters
and that helps me on the tough days when we can't talk. – Heather

127

They can't keep him forever – Irma

Our love for one another – Misty

Knowing that we are one day closer, whenever that day may be, to him coming home. – Stacey

Read or do anything to keep your mind off of the situation. – Jami

Some day it will all be over with. – Stephanie

I also asked some incarcerated mates this:

What positive words would you say to someone that was in your loved one's position of having a mate or family member that's incarcerated?

Never give up hope or listen to these people when they say to give up on your loved one. – Thomas

I understand that as life goes on our there, in here our lives are at a standstill, so a letter or answered phone call just means the world to us and makes us feel as if we still have some kind of importance in your life. – Anonymous

I would say to stay strong, and always keep the communication open. —
Anonymous

Stay strong! This is not going to be easy, but it will be worth it. — Anonymous

Be there for your person as much as possible. Being locked up is a different
world from the free world. — Jesse

Positivity, communication and honesty are very important during this journey. —
JB

I also asked a few recently released individuals this question.

What is the best support that friends and family members can give to their incarcerated loved ones?

Writing is the best way that you can support someone that's incarcerated. Write letters often. – Rhiannan

This too shall pass. This is only a stepping stone for a better future. If the incarcerated one has the strength, will power, and wants to be better for them, they can. While incarcerated, the inmate will be able to work on himself. There are usually classes to help with any situation. Therefore, your loved one will be able to handle situations in a civil manner. With strength and will power, your loved one will be able to strive to be a productive member in society. Also, pray to Jehovah God to help both of you to get through this time in your life as well as possible. It would be a good and needed idea to have a comfort zone for the inmate when they're released. When released its best to not bring up the past or hold a grudge with your loved one. Don't dwell on the past. Take one day at a time, and look into the positive things that will come out of this difficult time in both you and your loved one.

The biggest support during my incarceration was my family. The counselor and classes that I attended helped me to realize that if I believe, I can achieve. So with that being said, believing in myself helped me so much. When I started telling my family that I believed in myself, it helped them to believe in me also. Letters are good while incarcerated. I knew that when I was released I would be a better family member and friend. The words of encouragement from my family and a few friends that I still associated with helped me also. When someone believes in you, it makes you want to be a better person. Positive thought, positive feedback, and positive actions. That kept me going...along with my family. — Sabrena

Every day is a new day. Don't allow the bad ones to take you too far under.

Fill your mind with memories of your loved one, and pray for the best results

upon release. – Doug

For More Information

For more information or for support through your journey, please feel free to contact The Visiting Room. The Visiting Room is available on Facebook as well as their website.

FB.com/thevisitingroom

Thevisitingroom.org

Cover art was drawn by

Alex Garzes

Made in the USA
Columbia, SC
07 February 2018